TREATMENT IS NOT THE ANSWER TO DRUG ADDICTION!

Divine Secrets to Living a Drug-Free Life

DAMILOLA SUCCESS

WESTBOW
PRESS®
A DIVISION OF THOMAS NELSON
& ZONDERVAN

WestBow Press books may be ordered through booksellers or by contacting:

WestBow Press
A Division of Thomas Nelson & Zondervan
1663 Liberty Drive
Bloomington, IN 47403
www.westbowpress.com
1 (866) 928-1240

Scripture taken from the New King James Version®. Copyright © 1982 by Thomas Nelson. Used by permission. All rights reserved.

ISBN: 978-1-9736-7009-4 (sc)
ISBN: 978-1-9736-7010-0 (hc)
ISBN: 978-1-9736-7008-7 (e)

Library of Congress Control Number: 2019910679

Print information available on the last page.

WestBow Press rev. date: 08/15/2019

CONTENTS

INTRODUCTION

How in the world does anyone think treatment alone will get you off drugs? Ha-ha! You may be surprised that I laughed. I just laughed at the devil! Don't let anybody or any organization deceive you. There is no place on this planet—in drug addiction clinics or rehab centers—where addicts can completely get clean with ordinary treatment.

Do you think drugs can get you off drugs? That is a lie from the pits of hell. Treatment centers will only help you reduce the amount of drugs you're taking or are addicted to, and you can get addicted to government-approved drugs without realizing it. At the end of the day, you become an addict because the drug you're given in treatment centers to reduce your addiction are legally approved by the authorities. They say they'll *reduce*, not treat or get rid of your addiction. But they'll let you stay on some kind of drugs substituting what you were already using. You're still a drug addict, but now you're an addict on a legalized drug.

With my experiences in drug clinics over the past ten years, whether you're using legal or illegal drugs, many times the end result of addiction is death. The devil uses addiction as a means to reap people into his kingdom. We have to be conscious of his strategies and quickly take action.

What I want you to understand is that man is a spirit. He hailed from God, and as we know already, God is a spirit. We can't see Him, but He sees us and knows everything about us. Man is not just a body you are treating; he is beyond all that. It's high time we recognize that Our Spirit Man controls our body (i.e., our physical person, the one being treated).

If you don't treat your spirit man first, before your outward man, you are wasting your time. We all know time is precious in life; even the Bible says we should redeem our time.

The devil wants us to waste our time on earth—he wants us to be wandering about life without God, and waste all the money and time we're supposed to be using in sponsoring the gospel of our Lord Jesus Christ around the world. People want to be saved and enter the kingdom of God, but the devil wants us to waste that money on drug treatments and waste time on treatments that do not work.

In this book, I will share ways to get off drugs and beat your addiction so you can live a drug-free life without spending a penny.

You may ask how that can be possible. Nothing is impossible with God—well, if you believe. And when God does His thing, it's absolutely free, especially when He heals you from your drug addiction.

Chapter 1

YOUR HABIT

It's important to understand that you cultivated your addiction for a long period of time, and it has become part and parcel of who you are. Most of the time you become that habit. That means you become whatever you are addicted to, good or bad.

Good or bad, addiction is the result of a choice (i.e., choosing to use drugs in the first place). It cannot be imposed on a person, nor is it compulsory. Addiction is born from a habit; an addict unwittingly chose to use drugs for one reason or another. I said unwittingly because addicts didn't know they would become addicted to the substance they were using in the first place. Many assumed it would be just a "one-off" experience (some think they can handle the drug and won't become addicted).

Everyone has a story—whether terrible or good—that prompted them to the use of drugs for the first time. By using those substances, either to calm down or get high, the human body becomes addicted, and people cannot control or handle things in a natural way, especially when faced with life's challenges.

In a way, addicts become the drugs they were addicted to—you truly are what you eat, drink, and do. Addicts obsess over drugs, drugs, and more drugs. They can't concentrate on anything that could benefit them in a positive way. But remember, you're also what you think of every blessed day—if you think of evil ways, you become evil. If you think about goodness and good deeds, you're doing God's good work. It's a simple philosophy, but life is what you think of it.

Drug addicts look for "better" drugs than the one they're already addicted to, but the end result too often is death, because most drugs are poisonous to your system, and it becomes too much to handle. The fact is, many addicts know this. Their body function with the substance they are addicted to, so by trying to withdraw, they end up using some other drugs, ones they think are less harmful than the one they were using. Without them, they can't maintain their composure, Compare it to the gas in your car: without it, the car can't go anywhere or function properly. That is exactly what drugs do to the addict.

You're Exactly What You're Addicted To

For example, you don't need to advise an athlete to go for a walk; it's in his or her system. Likewise, if you are addicted to the word of God, you become the word because as the Bible says, as man thinks, so is he (Proverb 23:7 New King James Version). Man is exactly what he thinks about; no man is different from his thoughts.

It says in John 1:14 (NKJV), "And the word became flesh." This give insight that says if you are addicted to the word of God, it will become real in your life and make you what the word of God says. If you speak the word of God always, it will be real in your life. God spoke, and His words were real and physical; we can touch, feel, and smell them, and we are all enjoying them. Scientists are still discovering everything God said, and they can only see what He shows them.

Remember, we were made from the word of God, and if a man leaves that word out of his life, he will roam around in the circle of life without knowing where he is going, and he will never get anywhere, because life is a journey, and people have to know where they're journeying to.

Isn't it funny, and sad, that you're traveling yet not knowing the destination? It's like you bought a ticket on any flight and flew to wherever the plane landed without asking questions. You didn't bother asking because you don't know where you're going—you saw people boarding the same flight and assumed they must be heading someplace nice because there were pop stars, ministers, presidents, and well-respected society people—not to mention the professionals, businesspeople, politicians, lawyers, and lawmakers of the land. You see, they aren't *ordinary* people, according to the world system.

Your assumption put you in that line in the first place and made you conclude that you must be going to the right direction. But the truth is that you're not really sure of yourself. Everything started from your thoughts, which put you in that line in the first place!

It doesn't matter who is on your flight on the journey of life, whether the richest person or the poorest, or so-called wise men. What matters most is where you're going. Your destination is the most important thing; as the Bible says, the blind can't lead the blind. It doesn't matter how prominent a man might have been or how well respected in his community, what matters is how he is right now. His experiences don't count, because if people are spiritually blind, they will fall into a pit any time that kind of a person leads others.

We are too valuable to God to go astray or fall into a pit. His Son, Jesus, died for everyone. He didn't die because of mountains, hills, oceans, animals, birds, or for God's creations before man. Jesus died for you and me.

You can redirect your thinking back to the right line and board the right flight to take you to your destination. By so doing, you'll know exactly what you're doing, irrespective of anyone on the line because you know exactly where you're heading. Glory to God!

It is important that we have knowledge of something before we act on it, so we will know the consequences thereof. It's foolish to act in ignorance, because lack of knowledge destroys the soul, and there are no two ways about it: you need to find knowledge, no excuse.

How do you find knowledge? Simple: by asking the right questions. How do I know the right questions to ask? Be aware that nothing is new under the sun, and all the answers are in the Bible! The question you wanted to ask and the answers you seek are in the Bible. Someone else at some point already asked the question that is bothering your mind. It's up to you to do your research.

Success is personal, and not everyone is successful. Not everybody is a failure, though most fail in one aspect of life but are successful in another. But not everyone is successful in every aspect of life, as God wants us to be. God created everything we need and all we may want before He put us on this earth. I believe He did that for a reason. God put man in the middle of abundance, where there is no lack, and where we don't have to struggle for anything, not even drugs. The only reason man is not successful in the middle of this abundance is his lack of knowledge. He may be blinded spiritually, not seeing all the blessings of God around him.

This is very important. You need to allow God to open your spiritual eyes and see the importance of you. I never see a true successful man without God, for you to discover God; you will need to do your own personal research in His word by yourself.

Success is found through research and knowledge, and when you research, you acquires knowledge, which gives you wisdom, giving birth to real success. This applies to every areas of life. For example, it may be in your finances, family, business, and education—this principle can be applied to the drug addiction you want to break free from, or anything you're addicted to that's ruining your life.

Salvation Is Personal

You can choose to reign with Jesus in this world now and the world to come, or choose to stay on the other (Godless) side now and after this world comes to end times. You see, God will not force anyone to follow him; He is God, full of love. He wants you to make a choice for yourself, and He want you to choose Him.

He set before us life and death; He still said we should choose life, because he knew we have a tendency to choose death. He wants us to discover love through Him, so we can follow Him in spirit and in truth.

It's very important that you know God loves you, irrespective of any problem you might be facing. He created this whole world because of you, so you can enjoy your life to the fullest before you finally meet Him face-to-face.

Satan knows this, which is why he wants to manipulate people away from God using so many tricks. He has no new tricks, just the same lies he's been using since the beginning of the world, when Adam was created. He's still telling the same lies today.

God put you here, and He wants the best for you. He is too wise, too rich, and too full of love. He doesn't need anything from you apart from your love. He will teach you how to love genuinely.

The truth is that any other way, apart from the way of God (Jesus), is a complete waste of time. Jesus said, "I am the way and the truth and the life" (John 14:6 New International Version). Nobody ever said that before in any religion. He is not only the way to God the Father, but He is the way of life.

If you've never had Jesus as your way of life, I'm sorry, but nothing will truly work for you. Any other success, apart from the one in Jesus, will only go up to come down. It's just for a moment, but only the path of the just will shine brighter until they depart this world. Their success will be passed to their children and generation to come; it'll never run dry because it was found on the truth, the solid rock, Jesus Christ, God of everything.

Your Beliefs Will Not Change the Truth

What you have believed in your heart will not change the truth. Your own beliefs might be a lie, but I'm not saying they are. If what you believe is based on the word of God, it is surely the truth and not a lie.

You have held your beliefs for so many years because you inherited them from others or you held those thoughts as your own. The only true belief is based on the word of God, which is in Christ Jesus, and I am not ashamed to declare it. Nothing in this universe can change that truth, whether you believe it or not.

If you study the word of God, you will increase your knowledge, adding to what you've likely known since you were kid in Sunday school. Or maybe you haven't been to church in your life; it's never too late to learn about God. The Bible contains the word of God, but if you ignore the Bible, you can't really know God.

One of the reasons people don't know God is that they know too much science now, to the extent that they even want to prove that there is no God. Some people may not necessarily say there is no God, but their way of life indicates they believe in human intellect, not God. Those people run their own lives. For them,

God does not exist. When they're sick, they only believe in what the doctor says. Nothing else works for them, and when that knowledge fails them, they have no hope.

Drug addicts do the same thing: treatment fails them, so they have no hope apart from the treatment, and their knowledge limits them.

This is the reason for writing this book. I know with my experience in drug services, most addicts rely on the treatment that isn't working for them. They only get addicted to so many dangerous drugs out there, and the limitations of their thoughts and knowledge is killing them. They have no hope for tomorrow. They only depend on their treatment, and when someone dies, they think the guy just wasn't smart enough to beat the addiction. They didn't realize Satan is picking them one by one into his kingdom with his tricks.

When Satan chains you, he comes for you anytime he wants. It doesn't matter how smart you are—if you're in his chains, he'll kill you any time with anything. This is when you will see confused doctors. They will not know exactly what killed their patient and will only know that the patient shouldn't have died because he or she might have been responding well to treatment.

Because man is more than a physical body, treatment can only work when the spirit is sound and healthy, but when the spirit has been weak, no treatment will work. This is the truth a lot of people don't want to accept, especially ones who don't believe in any spiritual life. It's hard for a scientist or a doctor to believe in spirituality, except perhaps the ones who were Christians before they become doctors or scientists. All they see are what they work around, and they try to make us all believe that seeing is believing. I found the truth—that seeing is not believing—and discovered that what you see around you isn't all there is.

There's no way can we can get accurate results with merely our eyes. We will get wrong results that way, which can give birth to wrong decisions, wrong diagnoses, and wrong treatments. We need to upgrade our thinking with the word of God in order to know and experience the reality of life.

Chapter 2

YOUR THOUGHTS
DEFINE YOU

What do you think about? What are your thoughts? What are your meditations? I understood something must have happened before you ended up addicted to drugs. What do you see when you have problems or are emotionally down? Do you see yourself coming out of that problem? Or do you let people see for you? If you see yourself coming out of any problem at all, especially this drug addiction, this is the right book for you.

Or … if you're the type who, for any little challenge, consults your friends first to gather opinions in order to form your own, and you conclude that the majority carried the vote, as people say, it may be difficult for you to trust my advice.

The truth is, much of the time, the majority vote for the wrong person. In the end, they regret it. Because the majority don't know the truth, they only know the facts. Only a few seek for truth, and people think they are stupid.

God always uses something stupid in the eyes of men to perform His miracles. If not, how would you explain the rod Moses used to divide the Red Sea? It was unexplainable, according to science. So many miracles in biblical days don't make sense to human reasoning. Remember, not too many people are wise these days; the few wise ones get their wisdom from God, because He is wisdom personified. God is the only wise one, and for you to be wise, you need to know Him in His word.

There is no way you would reason God out of your head; the so-called majority gets their wisdom from someone's intellect, and the whole world believes and respects them and follows their footsteps.

People are often led astray by the majority when a hero they followed didn't know God, and it's difficult to change their thinking. Some believed if they changed their beliefs after a long time, people would think they're crazy, since their beliefs followed society's way of thinking, or even their family's belief systems. It doesn't matter whether the thought was wrong or right; no one cares to do research or ask questions. They live their lives the way they were taught. How sad that is!

You can't live your life according to your family's or society's beliefs if they go against your own. You need to cheek with the word of God whether you're living right, because there is only one God, and He is the only one we're going to give feedback to at the end of our lives here on earth. You are not accountable to anyone in life except to Him; if you are too conscious of what people say, that is what controls your life, negative or positive. Don't let the so-called majority dictate how you're going to live your life. Most of the time they failed, and no one heard about it.

Remember that the road that seems right to many is broad and leads to destruction. Only a few people get it right in life, and go follow a narrow path. The narrow way is just for a few people, not for all, so think about that!

It's not because God designs it that way, it's because most people want to live the way they learned from their family, society, or country. They don't want to find out if their way of living is right or wrong, and the only way to find out is to know God in His word.

The fact that you met life the way you met it doesn't mean it is the right way to live. You need to find out the truth and hold on to it. Then you will live a true life, regardless of what you met in your family, society, or country. There is only one God who everyone is going to give account to. God is not from many cultural backgrounds but is one God, one love.

If we need to improve things or change some stuff, we should do so. Not that we should stick to one doctrine even when we knew it's not improving us in any way. We can't keep saying it's been the rule or family policy for a long time. Any policies or doctrines that are not of God, be it in the family, town, country, or nations of the world, it is high time we change it before it changes us completely.

Some doctrines or policies were so devilish, Satan used them to deceive and destroy people from generation to generation, yet we still don't change them. This is the time for us to go for positive change; we can only change it through and by the word of God, and most especially with the help of the Holy Spirit. Glory to God!

My experience in drug addiction service made me realize that ordinary people don't see good things in drug addicts. What I meant by "ordinary people" are those with sense knowledge—all they see is what they believe, and seeing is not believing, as people say.

We believe God first and then see Him in again after we depart from our body. We can't say we're anxious to go to heaven before we can confirm that there is a God in heaven. God is a spirit. He lives in the spiritual realm, and we believe with our spirit because we are spirit. We are the image of God, not of angels or any other being; this whole physical world that we can actually see, touch, feel, and smell is controlled in the spiritual realm.

Just like in biblical days, when people thought good things could never come out of Nazareth (see John 1:46), but to their surprise, that was where our Lord Jesus Christ came from. Without Him life is a struggle, and no man can have peace. But with Him, life is easy and sweet like honey. Every drug addict can have good life and live a drug-free life with a great future ahead. There is so much potential for some addicts I have met over the past eleven years. All they need is someone to help them discover their potential, someone to show them the love of God and teach them the real treatment they're looking for.

But you can't access this treatment without experiencing the real love of God. This treatment is what I call "natural treatment," which will enable them to be totally free from drug use or abuse. This treatment is different from anything provided in any system used for drug addicts. This natural treatment changes the entire thinking system and gives addicts a sense of self-worth. It adds so much value to them, so they will see a great future ahead.

According to my research, the whole idea of drug treatment is not working; addicts are dying every day from overdoses. Even the so-called treatment centers barely let them exist, not really wanting them off drugs, because if they do, the government loses a lot of money on the treatments (drugs) they're giving the addicts.

The truth is there's nothing like permanent treatment in any drug treatment center. The whole idea of drug treatment clinics geared toward addicts is just a way to reduce their intake of different drugs they were addicted to, but it's still another way to get them addicted to other licensed drugs that were approved by the state.

Our eyes are limited and cannot see everything around us. We need spiritual eyes to see the truth, be it in our lives, our families, or our nation. This is my reason for the natural treatment, to cure any kind of addiction, especially drug addiction.

Some addicts have been stamped in the spirit world, and Satan took advantage of their bad habit. He chained them with that drug habit because they chose to go down that road; you see, the devil cannot force anybody to do his will, but he has so many tricks to direct you away from what God has planned for you. Satan knew God only has good plans for you, even before you were formed in your mother's womb, so Satan targets that plan to destroy it, and this is the reason it's easy for Satan to use your bad habit to destroy you, and you will think it's merely addiction.

Satan, a spirit being, causes something to happen in this physical world to your body. Do you now think the treatment you are taking will give you the answer you really want? Think about this. Imagine someone you cannot see physically has made your life miserable and it is costing you a lot of money, time, or emotional trauma. Your life is a deep mess, and you can't do anything reasonable with your life. Yet you're a spirit and cannot see him because you're in a physical body, which is terrestrial. You can't relate to the person physically at all, and the person hates you with passion. What do you think you will or can do? Think about this for a moment.

I think you should take the high road; it's obvious the guy wants you dead. You don't need to beg him; there's no need for any argument, nor is there any need for dialogue in order to settle. Note this: you don't dialogue with the devil. He isn't worth it; it's a complete waste of time. What you need to do is to find a strategy to pin him down before he catches you, and put him where he belongs. You need to find a way of winning by all means and at all costs, because the devil want to destroy you with your addiction; therefore, losing is not an option.

Remember, Satan is a spirit. You have to put him under your feet where he belongs. You need not be afraid of him because he has no power, and he doesn't want you to know your weight in Christ so that he can manipulate you the way he wants.

This made me derive a natural way of winning, which I call a natural way to treat drug addiction. You need to go into the spirit to deal with your addiction; I always say spirit first before doing anything successful in the physical world.

When you go into the spirit to pin Satan down and put him under your feet where he belongs, he'll have no power over you ever again. You'll see yourself walk away from drug addiction no matter how deeply you've gone or how many years you've been addicted.

You'll walk out without any protocol or counseling, and it will happen the way you don't expect. You don't even have to pay for it, and the beautiful thing is, you will begin to testify about how you walked out of treatment and left addiction behind.

This natural process is simple and powerful, but a lot of people don't recognize it. Those who knew about it ignored it and had no respect for it. It will be wise for you to take the word of the wise and follow it if you really want to break free from addiction. No other wisdom from men could work if it wasn't found through the word of God. Only the word of God, plus your own faith, can heal you from addiction. Having faith in God is very important, because without faith, nothing can work for you. Your cooperation with God is vital, and you will easily succeeded in breaking the chains of addiction through this natural process I will describe in the next chapter.

Chapter 3
Natural Treatment

It's understood that anything that comes naturally tends to last longer and have no side effects because it's natural. For example, giving birth naturally is far better than Caesarean section. Though the natural way of giving birth may be painful and inconvenient, it's still the best way because it is natural and there's usually a quick recovery. That is how God wants it. Likewise, the natural way of leaving drugs behind is the best way, with few side effect.

Addicts get better and even more glorious than they were using this natural treatment. It's very simple and free, but it requires your time. You need to devote quality time to this treatment every day, until you're totally free from even the craving of any kind of drugs.

Your mind has to be focused on picturing yourself drug-free. Zechariah 4:6 (NKJV) said, "'Not by might nor by power, but by my Spirit,' says the LORD of hosts." Handling the natural way of treatment will not be you alone; you need the Holy Spirit to help you. This is the reason for going for treatment in an addiction clinic in the first place, because you're looking for help, but you're getting the help that's not working for you—you just don't know it yet.

Some people have been in and out of treatment for fifteen to twenty years. They repeat the same treatment, take the same medications, and get stuck. They can't stop going; it's like they'll be on that medication for the rest of their lives if care isn't taken. I have to ask myself: Is drug treatment like a terminal illness?

The sad thing is that people won't know that it's going to be the end of their life just like that. They thought they wanted to feel high once more and enjoy the moment, but unfortunately, it doesn't always go the way they think.

I wondered when they would finally be free and live the normal life God intended for them, but Satan cheats them with addiction. This got my attention, and I started looking for ways to help any addict I met.

Ever since I joined an addiction clinic—more than ten years now—I haven't seen a single person come out of drug addiction successfully with this treatment, but I have seen a lot of death, which is unspeakable.

People got addicted to government-approved drugs, although in their minds, they think they're doing well. But they're not! The substitute drugs the doctor prescribed for them was like a life handcuff with no key. Even those doctors who locked the handcuff cannot open it. The Spirit of God made me have a special interest in drug addicts, and God made me see every addict differently. I see the beauty of God in them.

Not that I was on drugs; I never saw drugs until I studied addiction. It's the love of God in my heart that makes me see what God sees in addicts. This made me want to help them in many ways, but the policy of my workplace won't permit me to practice my natural treatment. This is the main reason I wrote this book, and I hope it helps someone to become drug-free no matter the circumstances.

Holy Spirit is the only helper for drug addiction treatment. When it comes to treatment, you cannot ignore Him. If you trust Holy Spirit for so many things in your life but don't trust Him enough for whatever addiction you're battling, then you don't know Him enough.

There's a pain in my heart any time I walk into the clinic where I work and hear that a client who was healthy yesterday died of an overdose overnight. My heart sinks when I hear that kind of news. It baffles me, and I mourn in my spirit. I believe they needed help that is beyond these treatments.

The Spirit of God had made me see them differently; I see the beauty of God in each and every one of them. I see where they ought to be and where they are now.

I know God's plan for them, and I saw what the devil made them become. God made me see every addict in a very special way that ordinary men do not see. Mere men don't see anything special in drug addicts; they always think it is their fault. I don't mean to be rude, readers; my own definition of "mere men" are people who don't believe in Holy Spirit; they don't accept Him; therefore, a person is not born again, even though he might be a Christian for so many years.

Ordinary people who do not believe in the supernatural power of God adore only what they can see, feel, or taste, anything other than that they throw it in the trash. Ordinary people (or mere men) see things the way everybody sees and view the way everybody views. But few of us view differently because of the Holy Ghost. Glory to God!

Holy Spirit had helped me to see God in every drug addict, and that is my reason for declaring through this book that *treatment is not the best answer for drug addiction.* I know it's not 100 percent their fault to be addicted to drugs, it is beyond all that, and the so-called medical treatment is *not working.*

When you diagnose correctly, you know the exact treatment to prescribe. But when you're not sure about the diagnosis, you guess which drug to prescribe, which is the beginning of a patient's trouble. A lot of people are in this situation, especially drug addicts, but they don't know because they trusted their physician. And at the end, if anything goes wrong, they blame their physician for everything. A lot of addicts even blame their doctors for simple things they were supposed to be responsible for during their treatment, such as keeping appointments. How do you expect to be helped if you can't respond to the help people offer? Your roll in this is very important to make you free from drug addiction.

Your Response Is Very Important

The Bible says we should meditate on the word of God every time, day and night. The Lord God declares a sovereign declaration to Joshua, that "This Book of the Law shall not depart from your mouth" (Joshua 1:8 (NKJV). That declaration is for every living soul on earth, that you, "the addicts," should meditate in that law, which is the word of God, day and night, and you will make your way prosperous and will have good success.

This is a very simple but powerful way to break free from drug addiction, and it's important you achieve that goal. Notice something remarkable in that verse: all the responsibilities are yours. You have to do the meditations yourself, not the Holy Spirit this time, not your parent, your spouse, or your children. It's nobody else's responsibility because you're the one who needs to be free from addiction.

That means you have to do the meditation yourself. Remember, according to Joshua 1:8 (NKJV), "This Book of the Law shall not depart from your mouth, but you shall meditate in it day and night, that you may observe to do according to all that is written in it. For then you will make your way prosperous, and then you will have good success."

This is the only thing that works in the whole wide world, not treatment alone! But you need to take that responsibility for yourself with the help of the Holy Spirit, because the word of God never fails.

Take Responsibility for Yourself

If you are sixteen or older, you need to know you're responsible for whatever action you take or decision you make. Don't blame your parents, family, spouse, or environment for your own personal actions, because none of those people will suffer the consequences but you. To be a drug-free person, you need to know and accept that you are responsible for yourself.

If you can accept this simple fact and run with it, it's better for you because every drug addict blames everyone, everything, and everywhere for their drug abuse and always run away from the truth. Delete anybody or anything that you blame for causing your addiction. Delete them from your mind, and focus. I know you will ask, how is that possible? Yes, it's possible.

Now, I want you to imagine you're the only one in your world, and you want to make good things happen for yourself. You want to live a good life. If you have this mentality that you can do anything, you know that any help you get from someone else will be like a jackpot or additional advice. You may use it or choose to ignore it because you don't really rely on them. You may have already made up your mind that you're not going to totally depend on people, because if you do, you may be disappointed.

The truth is, nobody but you is under any obligation to make you clean from drugs. Once you accept that fact in your mind, all things are possible unto you; it will be so easy to live a drug-free life.

I don't in any way condemn treatment centers or rehab clinics. Their intentions are good but aren't working the way they thought it would. In essence, I believe it can't work on its own; only the word of God can work on its own.

There's something more to drug treatment that addiction clinics can't easily discover. We're dealing with drug addiction treatment here, not treatment of a headache or fever. This is a psychological and mental sickness and a bad-habit sickness. In fact, I know some prominent professionals who can't do anything without using drugs. It's become part of their ritual every day before going to work. They can't carry out their normal duties without using drugs; these people are not junkies, because a lot of people think it's only the junkies who are mainly addicted to drugs. When you talk about drugs, people first think about homeless junkies roaming about the street, whereas the main drug abusers are professionals.

I have seen professionals who can't do without heroin, Some are addicted to cocaine, and they know how to use it well, to the extent that they can't be easily suspected, they are so expert in using their drug use.

People think they have confidence in carrying out their respective duties on their job, but unfortunately it's not true, because when drugs are at work, people become exposed. It's a matter of time before their addiction catches up with them and affects work performance.

Drugs are expensive, and people living on the streets can't really afford them the way people think. Those on social welfare can't afford heroin or cocaine every time; in fact, that's one of their reasons for joining addiction clinics, to get methadone, the heroin replacement, for free. For many addicts, their income isn't enough to feed them and pay their bills, let alone buy drugs on the street. This is the reason all kinds of bad behavior go hand-in-hand with drug addiction,

Those on social welfare are not really the main drug addicts, according to my research and experience. They are like an errand boys to the main drug dealers. I also discovered that dealers are not necessarily addicts, though many use drugs occasionally. They want to make quick money, and some don't use drugs at all. That shocked me.

The aim of drug dealers is that you lose your head while they make money on you, they don't care, and they think business is business no matter what, even if it costs somebody's life. They don't care; all they want is money.

The main drug addicts are professionals, some movie/music stars in a circular world, some politicians, some athletes, etc.; not all, but some of the most famous ones, because most of them that are not in Christ (not born-again Christians). Or maybe they are born again, but they don't really know who they are in Christ. Those are the ones who tend to get addicted to one drug or another.

Most of their reason for using drugs is to be able to face the crowd during the course of their profession because their spirit is not trained to face a crowd, only their body was trained, so they use drugs to cover up to be bold enough to deliver their jobs. It doesn't matter whether it's your doctor, or your own career, your key worker, or your probationer officer who is helping you get off drugs; most of them are struggling with their own issues too.

I said earlier that addiction is a psychological and mental sickness. Everything may look good on the outside, but on the inside they struggle to even live sometimes. The feeling is the same, but only their statuses are different. Once you get yourself addicted, it's not good for your health.

Imagine relying on this kind of person to take care of your addiction, when they can't deal with their own. They end up saying that everybody is addicted to one thing or another, as if you were meant to be addicted to a substance, which I found to be a lie. It's a deception by Satan to hook you with your bad habit. It's not meant to be like that; it's your choice. Addictions destroy lives; only addiction to the word of God can make you a success.

The reason those addicts still manage to go to work and do what they do is to pay their bills. They don't really enjoy life the way people think. They struggle so much on the inside, and people still meet them for help they can't really give. Some of them are the doctors you are looking for; some are celebrities with the kind of luxurious lifestyles that people wish they could live.

Don't get me wrong; there is nothing wrong with living luxuriously, but don't use drugs to cover up your inabilities, because God even wants us to live our best for Him. People looking at those pop stars from afar don't really know that there are lots of messes and untidy lives going on on the inside.

Forget about the nice suits and makeup, drug addicts suffer the same things psychologically and mentally. The only different is that one might have a house and family and the other might be living on the street, homeless, possibly on welfare.

Even the ones with a house and family now may lose them to drugs later, if care is not taken. Life with drugs doesn't guarantee a good stable life. There is a best life that God has planned for every one of us.

Using drugs to solve temporary problems or challenges is very dangerous. You can't find permanent solutions that way. You can lose everything you work for in life within a short period of time. Whether it's legal or illegal drugs, prescribed or unprescribed, a drug is a drug, and addiction isn't different either. Once addicted, you're an addict. It doesn't matter if it's heroin, cocaine, morphine, methadone, or Percocet. Satan doesn't care what you're addicted to. He wants to use that drug to destroy you completely. Satan doesn't have any future; therefore, he doesn't want anyone to have one either.

Satan's ambition for drug addicts is to destroy them. He does not have any future for them; he has locked them up through the treatment in addiction clinics and rehab centers. That is the reason you see people in treatment for more than ten years, because these clinics don't know how to go about the addiction treatment; they only replace drugs with drugs.

No drug addicts intended to stay in treatment for ten years. They came for help to overcome their addiction, but by introducing another drug to them, they stay longer than they should. Before they know it, ten years pass and nothing happened. They only get more addicted to so-called prescribed drugs and still crave the heroin or cocaine they were addicted to before.

Someone told me he started on ten mg of methadone and has been taking it for fifteen years now; he doesn't know how to come off the prescription medication. Instead of finishing his drug rehab, as he was expecting, he suddenly got worse. He doesn't know how he ended up taking 120 mg all these years later. He was getting cleaned up but got worse again, and doctors don't have a clear explanation for that other than to blame the addict who is looking for help.

The only thing addicts get from long-term treatment is different kinds of disease in their bodies, such as kidney failure, heart disease, lung problems, teeth problems, and infections.

This is what Satan wants from your drug treatment—not a cure. Satan's plan is to use that clinic to deceive as many people as he wants, and then they get stuck in treatment, because he knows they will never overcome their addiction that way.

Satan knows he's slapped handcuffs on so many addicts the moment they enter the clinic, because addicts will be introduced to other treatment drugs, which they have to take daily. They're expected to be stable on these new replacement drugs, taking them instead of whatever they were addicted to.

But this treatment doesn't stop them from craving the original drug, and they continue using their old drugs and come to the clinic for the new ones. For example, heroin addicts show up for methadone(a government-approved drug), which replaces the heroin, Addicts are allowed to take methadone every day instead of heroin. But in my experience, many addicts take both drugs, which sometimes results in an overdose; they register at the clinic for official purposes because they have to in order to get their prescribed medication.

Only few of drug addicts get clean through rehab clinics, and those few happen through God's Grace, not only by the treatment they get from the clinics. Others die miserable deaths, either by overdose or suicide, which are part of the devil's tricks to get them. Because if someone is in treatment for so long, there is a tendency that he or she will overdose or commit suicide if the person doesn't get the right help.

Sometimes addicts are frustrated to the point of attempting suicide because they know they're not making progress, and the devil plays with their minds; he keeps telling them they're worthless, that nothing good can come from their lives. So they dance to the tune of the devil and try suicide by overdosing or doing self-harm.

Imagine going to see a priest and confessing that you're a thief. You want him to talk to God on your behalf to forgive you, not knowing the priest is also stealing from the offering plate. Your intention is good and is right in the sight of God, but that priest is not going to help you; he will indirectly teach you how to be an expert in stealing without being caught if you have a close relationship with him. Because he is also a thief, he can't talk to God for you. He can only teach you what he knows.

It's the same when you're being treated by a doctor who is also a drug addict. You're going to get the wrong advice from him, plus the wrong prescription, because he has not helped himself, and both of you are addicts. It doesn't matter if your doctor calls his own drug "a medication" for any kind of ailment in his body, once he is addicted to it and doesn't know how to overcome it, he is bound to it and is also an addict. Then how will he help you?

Satan has chained both of you with addiction of drugs. It is wise to think that someone sitting down can't lift up people who are lying on the floor. Only those people who are standing up straight can lift people who are lying on the floor.

Addiction clinics will not provide treatment for overdosing or attempting suicide; they only give you a drug to substitute the one you were addicted to. For an addict to come off prescribed drugs, it has to be done by the special grace of God, and strong determination, because people think doctors are a second God, especially when it is comes to addiction treatment. They trust doctors more than God, even when the Bible says you should trust God with your life. Don't lean on your own understanding, including a doctor's understanding, because when you do, it is a sure road for failure. There's no doubt about it.

I didn't say not to take your doctor's advice, but don't lean on it. *Doctors are not God.* They can only try, but they can't fix anything wrong with you mentally or psychologically, especially when it comes to drug addiction treatment. Remember, this is what drug treatment is all about: your mind first, and then your physical body.

Sadly, the end for a drug addict can be untimely death; their death can be so sudden and so premature, it is often painful and unexpected. It brings so much pain to the families of the addict that can never be forgotten. The most painful part is that it's women who suffer the most pain emotionally because she is the mother of the addict; she is the one who gave birth to them. The pain isn't the same emotionally for fathers because they don't get pregnant, so the feelings and the pain are totally different, and their attitude toward the addict is also different.

I didn't say fathers too don't feel the pains; don't get me wrong; of course they feel it, because they love their children too. What I'm trying to say is that mothers suffer a lot more emotionally than do the fathers. Sometimes she cannot discuss or disclose the pain to people, especially when she sees her child doing drugs and thinks she can't control the situation or do anything about it. The feelings with the fathers are not always the same, and I think that is how God created them. Women seem to care and worry more about their children than men do. Anyway, what I'm trying to stress is that whether you are a professional drug addict or unprofessional drug addict, the only way you can be drug-free is to totally believe in God and His word.

Believe in yourself, because when you trust God and believe in yourself that you can do all things, that is when you take responsibility of your life. This is exactly what God is looking for in us: people who will totally trust Him with everything and believe in themselves, and not trust in their own strength but in God's.

Remember David in the Bible. He had confidence in the Lord, and that was how he was able to defeat his enemy. The God of David then has not changed. He is still the same today and will be forever, so accept and trust only Him.

What I want you to realize is that you can't do it all by yourself. Without God and His word, which are one, we are no different from our word.

Chapter 4

Don't Kick God Out!

Never kick God out of your life, because if you do, you'll struggle with the treatment you're receiving and may even find yourself going on and off the treatment. You may be tempted to use additional drugs besides the prescribed one you're receiving in the clinic. This is dangerous because abusing drugs can cause an untimely death through misuse or overdose. In searching for better and cheaper drugs outside the clinic, combined with the treatment you're receiving, there is a risk that you could die. All those combined drugs could cause medical conditions, including heart problems, and this is a sad way to live.

Getting addicted to the prescription drugs is bad as well. Before you know what's happening, you've spent ten-plus years in treatment, which has then become a lifestyle, a routine in your life, which is abnormal and a wrong way to live. You can't continue like that! God didn't create you to live on drugs, no matter what the situation is or what might have happened to you. He created you to live on and for Him; He created you to show His beauty and the glory in this world. Remember, you were created by the word of God, and your whole being (your spirit, soul, and body) was made by the word of God, which means God made and owns you. He is the only one who can fix anything that has gone wrong in your spirit, soul and body. He is a Spirit; He knows all. (For example, a computer manufacturer knows what he put together to make that computer work perfectly. If anything goes wrong, it's better to look at the manual to see how to fix it, instead of trying to guess.)

It's the same with God. He knows all about you, what you cannot discuss with anyone, including your doctor; He knows what you're going through, even though He still wants you to come close to Him and tell Him your problems. He's ready and willing to hear you and solve your problems once and for all.

Don't say, "If God knows what I'm going through, why doesn't He fix it?" He's supposed to at least have mercy on you, because as I said, He loves you. But he doesn't work that way—you can't ignore your father and expect him to give you what you need. You need to come close to Him and ask for what you need, even though He already knows. God demands our attention so that we can live our best lives. He knows that when you come close to Him, you're too much for the devil to rattle. Satan can't come near your territory.

Drug addiction is a distraction from the devil to waste away life, so you only live for drugs instead of God. It's a big distraction that will make you think God doesn't exist. But I tell you, it's a trick the devil uses to pin you down. God exists. We exist for Him, and He is the only one you can actually turn to to solve your addiction.

God Can Solve Your Drug Problem

You may be wondering, what does God have to do with drug treatment? The Bible says every good gift is from God. Drug addiction is definitely not from Him; all bad behaviors are from Satan. There is nothing good about Satan. He is the father of all lies. He will lie to you to stay in treatment, and at the same time, he will deceive you to use extra drugs outside your treatment program so you can overdose, just to get rid of you. Satan doesn't have anything good to offer. His ultimate goal is to destroy you, nothing else. What I discovered is that Satan has been using the so-called rehab treatment to destroy youngsters; he uses it to destroy families, because they depend on drug treatment.

Satan made addicts stay in the treatment for so long to the extent that people inherited drugs as they were growing up, and he uses that to destroy families from one generation to another. We need to be conscious of the truth that getting addicted to drugs has no good end. It's Satan's deception to rip people off into his kingdom, and it's not going to get better the way things are going right now, with all the treatments established by the government all over the world.

This is the reason I want you, my brothers and sisters who are addicted to one kind of drug or the other, to trust God with your life; yes, I call you my brothers and sisters because we all came from one God. Don't rest on human knowledge, including the treatment you're getting at the moment. Don't put your life into your doctor's hands, as if the doctor is your maker. They don't own you; they can only try, with all their guesses, to reduce your addiction to the substance you were using, not to completely take you off that substance.

Always remember that doctors have their limits. Some of them have their own struggles under their suits, including the drug addiction you went to see them for; you thought they would be able to help you, but it's not always what you think. I found that people look at those doctors as their savior, especially when they are trying to overcome addiction. Don't look at them like your savior. They are only human, like you. I mentioned earlier that some might also be addicted to drugs as well.

An addict is an addict. It doesn't matter what kind of drugs. Respect your doctor's knowledge. At least he or she will try to reduce your drug intake. Your intention for going to the doctor in the first place was to help you focus, and that can help make you drug free.

At least something motivated you on your inside to register for an addiction clinic, which I believe is God in you, because you're looking for help. I know the devil doesn't have any good advice to give anybody; he can't tell you to look for treatment. He wants you to die with no help. All he knows is to destroy, nothing else. The intent that makes you want to be drug free is very important; I believe the intension comes from God.

Feed your spirit with positive words. As I said earlier, I see God in every drug addict. God owns you, He is the owner and the manufacturer of you, and He is your maker. God is the only one who can fix anything that goes wrong in your life. Satan does not own anyone, so believe that you give yourself to him because of your ignorance.

Don't be in the dark anymore. Come to the light of God. God can be your best friend if you let Him, and He will fix everything for you for free. But it's not possible without Jesus. Don't say, "I believe in God, but I don't believe in Jesus." Jesus is the way to God; let no one deceive you that you can talk to God or have a relationship with God without Jesus and the Holy Spirit.

Jesus said, "I am the way, the truth, and the life. No one comes to the Father except through me" (John 14:6 NIV). Things and beings were made by Him. He owns everything and anything. The bible says in John1:3 that all things were made by Him, and without Him, nothing was made. That means no one can do something permanently right except by Him.

No solution anywhere, every other solution is temporal, and for a short period of time, so you should expect the worst after that, if you choose a temporary solution. No one on this planet can have a true relationship with God except through Jesus Christ. It doesn't matter how many times you pray in a day or how long you stay in meditation. What you meditate on matters a lot. If your meditation is not about Jesus or His word, any other meditation prescribed as part of your drug treatment is not going to get you off drugs. It doesn't matter how many hours you spent on it, it's not going to work.

Don't be deceived by any of the so-called professional counselors who do not know the Holy Spirit. Holy spirit is the best counselor on this planet. And if you don't know Jesus, you can't know God. Jesus is the way to real life. He is the true life and the true way of life. He is life itself, and I'm sure that if you have Him in your life, you already know the truth and can't go wrong in life. This is when your real life begins. But prior to this, you are a cheap meat for the devil to catch.

Any other ways are lies from the pits of hell. It doesn't matter who your mentor was or is right now, or who inspires you in life; if the person doesn't show you Jesus, who is the real way, the real life, and the absolute truth, it's like the blind leading the blind. And everyone who follows, including the leader, will fall into the pits of hell. No doubt about it—that is exactly what the devil wants.

This is a simple truth, and as simple as it is, people hate to hear it. but I have to say the truth, Don't say, "Here come the religion folks again, trying to tell us what to do!" No! The fact is, you have known a lot before I met you, and what you knew didn't cure you from drug addiction. Now that you're reading my book, why don't you try my wisdom? That's if you're really sure you want to be drug free. At least there's no harm in it—you're discovering new knowledge, which is very simple but powerful.

Don't say, "Who does she think she is, trying to share her own wisdom?" Yeah! You see my wisdom is from God, the Father of Abraham, Isaac, and Israel. He is my Father by my faith in Jesus Christ. God has opened my eyes to see how special every drug addict is. I saw bundles of formerly successful people after Satan replaced their success with failure, destroying them every day through drugs. Sometimes when I walk around in Dublin, where I reside, and I see a drug addict, he or she might be sleeping rough at that moment; God will quickly show me how successful he or she ought to be.

I found that, when talking with them, that some are from Christian homes. Some love God, but they don't know how to serve Him. They think they are too dirty for God to hear them. Some will say to me that when they get clean they will serve God, thinking that that's when God can answer their prayers. Some don't have a clue who God is. They say something like, "If God is real, why did He allow me to become addicted?" Some said they've been praying to God to take this addiction away, that they stick to the rules and regulations of the clinic and pray every night, only to find that, after being clean for a few months or even a couple of years, they somehow found themselves back on drugs, now even worse than when they first started.

The truth of the matter is that anybody can pray if they want. You can pray every hour if you like. But the question is, is God hearing you? Do you know Him through Jesus? Or do you know God from afar? Maybe you know God is in heaven, and one day He will come and help you with all your suffering if He is willing.

I met people told me that they know God is in heaven; they pray to Him every night, and they know that one day he will send His angels to help them with their drug addiction. If He doesn't, that means it's their lot in life, meaning God is not willing.

Some said they worship gods, and if they ask their gods to do something for them or to protect them in any way, and something terrible happens after, they believe that means the gods are not willing at that time, and they have to try again some other day to appeal to the gods.

Some people even told me drug addiction was their destiny because they grew up with a parent using drug. They said if there is a God, the way I told them He loves them, why did He throw them into a family of drug users? You see how the devil has manipulated people's minds, twisting them to believe there is no God? The devil has brainwashed so many drug addicts like that.

I still maintain that God really loves them. Any time I am faced with questions from drug abusers, I let them know there is a God in heaven, that He sees them more than they see themselves. His love is unconditional; nobody can love them the way He does.

You may also believe in many gods like the people I have met, but the truth is that any other god, apart from the one who owns the whole universe, God Almighty, who came as flesh as Jesus, any other god can't help you. You're wasting your time because they are all God's handywork. Men chose to worship them, but they can't ever be God.

The physical life we live here on earth is controlled from somewhere that we need to know about, which many call "the spirit world." Bad habits are controlled from the spirit realm, so I don't blame you for not getting it right now. At least you've tried all you could and are still getting the same results. But there is something more to life that you don't know, especially about drug addiction. Drug addiction can be controlled from the spirit world for positive or negative change, depending on what you choose.

Chapter 5

LIFE IS SPIRITUAL

Every move in life is controlled by the unseen world, which is the spirit world. Both good and bad moves came from there. You may not know this, but your ignorance does not change this truth. The spirit world controls the physical world, and anything you're doing here on earth has been controlled by the spirit world.

Everything you see with your physical eyes isn't all there is. You can't see everything with just physical eyes—you need to open your eyes to the spirit world to be able to know what is happening around you.

This drug addiction you're battling? You may not know why the treatment hasn't been working for you. It may have been decided in the spirit realm that you will live addicted to drugs, and if that's the case, you may be on drugs for the rest of your life. You need to find out why and how you are the way you are, especially those who were born into a drug-abusing family.

Anything like this is definitely from the devil and not from God. The Bible says every good and perfect gift come from God (James 1:17). Anything you choose to do has the seal of the spirit in it, and God has given us the ability to choose. He won't force us; He said we should choose between life and death, and He even told us to "choose life" because He knew we would choose death.

All things that have been concluded in the spirit world are made manifest in the physical. And that is what governs all the behavior you see in this world today. For example, the killing of Christians all around the world has been concluded in the spirit realm by the devil and his angels, and he uses non-Christians to execute his mission. Even some of the atrocities people commit today are so bad, you might wonder whether the people who committed the sin were even human. Even an animal, if not used by the devil, would never commit such a crime. Some criminal cases are so bad that whenever you hear about them, you feel sick. You're left thinking that even life in jail or death can't solve the damage that's been done.

It's only when you have the spirit of God in you that you will know that devil and his demons have carried out their business. The same thing applies to drug addiction. You're battling with the devil, and he may have signed up your bad habit and handcuffed you with it over a long period of time. He doesn't have any power over anyone and can't force you to do anything except give yourself to him through your habit.

Remember, he is the author of all the bad habits on earth; he does not have anything good to offer. And if you're going to shut down the devil and his demons, you need to know Jesus. No two ways about it!

I am writing this book for people who are desperately ready to break the handcuffs of drug addiction—those whose hands are tied and really want to break free.

Those people must have come to the conclusion that they are responsible for the kind of life they are living at the moment, and they need to change their life for the better. These people have stop blaming everybody for their lifestyle or for their habit—be yourself, take up your own cross, and face reality.

The reality is to know Jesus and receive the Holy Spirit; the Holy Spirit is the real helper for drug treatment. You see, He doesn't live in the sense realm. You need to know Jesus, receive and accept Him by faith, before you have that connection with the Holy Spirit. When you do that, life is no more a mystery to you; you step into your real life, and things will work out to your advantage. Don't say religious folks don't have a clue what drug addiction is.

Yes, I know what I'm talking about, with my experience for the past ten years working with drug addicts. I could have written a book every year over the last ten years to show you that I really know what am talking about regarding drug addiction. All I'm saying is that no standard treatment works for drug addiction— this I'm sure of. I suggest you try Jesus and see what the outcome will be; it's very simple, and it costs nothing. I'm sure you will come back to testify!

It's Simple with Jesus

Drug addiction is the simplest of all the problems Jesus can solve; it is simple with Him.

Take a look at the life of Jesus. Whenever He met anyone with a problem, He solved the matter through the simplest way possible. He said to the blind man that his faith made him whole; the blind man opened his eyes and saw, just like that, with no sacrifice. Jesus did not require anything from him; He asked, "What do you want?" And the man said, "I want to see," and Jesus said, "Then open your eyes."

It's so simple with Jesus. The same thing happened with the woman with the issue of blood. She came out to touch Jesus with faith, and Jesus asked, "Who touched me?" The woman said she did. Jesus already knew why the woman touched Him. She came out with no shame among the crowd and told the truth. Jesus said again, "Your faith has made you whole." You see that it's very simple with Jesus—no sacrifice, no payment, and no prescriptions required.

Look at that woman with the issue of blood, who was not ashamed of the crowed, especially what people said about her. She was tired of her predicament, was even broke as a result, and there was no money to visit doctors, as the Bible described. She didn't care about the people around her; she'd made up her mind that if she could just touch the hem of Jesus's garment, that will be end of her sorrow. You can read her story in Mathew 9:20–22.

She took responsibility upon herself and didn't wait for any pastor to pray for her, nor did she blame anybody for not helping her situation. She doesn't feel sorry for herself; she rose up in great faith and took the risk of coming out in the crowed to do what she had to do, and she was free forever, living happily ever after.

The same is with drug addiction. You can be free and live happily forever without any trace of an addiction. The Bible says in Jeremiah 17:7 (NKJV), "Blessed is the man who trusts in the Lord, and whose hope is the Lord." You see, if you put 100 percent of your hope in the Lord and don't doubt His power, there is no mountain too high for you to climb.

Drug addiction is the cheapest and easiest among mountains, though people are ignorant of this truth. It is not a big deal to at least have a little faith in the power of God; you will be surprised by what that faith can achieve. You don't need to spend the rest of your life in drug treatment; tiny faith like a muster seed can free you from drug addiction forever.

I have told you earlier that the number-one treatment is to believe in God. Put your hope in God, not your doctor. I love the Amplified Bible (AMP) version of the verse I mention above, Jeremiah 17:7. It says, "Blessed [with spiritual security] is the man who believes *and* trusts in *and* relies on the Lord, and whose hope *and* confident expectation is the Lord."

You see, you can trust men and not rely on them, but on the other hand, you can trust men but not really have confidence in them for all things, because if you trust and rely on men for any reason at all, one day they're going to show you what they're made of. God knew what man was made of, because He made them. He already knows how he functions and knows how he will end his life. You only know how man is functioning now; you don't know what he is going to do next, but God knows all.

That is the reason He want you to trust Him with your life—rely on and have confidence in Him. You will never be disappointed in any way. God is not a man that He should lie. He wants you to expect all your expectations from Him. Trust Him with anything and everything you require for life and godliness. He wants you to ask Him, and He will give it to you with love. When someone gives you a gift with love, it is different from the gift you collected without love. You will never forget the one you collected with love and will even tell your friends about it because you will always remember it.

This is how God works. His name is love, and He gives everything to you with love. He loves us so much so that He gave Himself for us, no one can do that! What will He not give you?

Be conscious of the truth that God owns you; He is your maker, and He is the only one who can fix anything that goes wrong in your life in any circumstances.

Don't put your confidence in your doctor, and don't rely on him as though he is responsible for your well-being. No! You are responsible for your own happiness. Doctors are only going to prescribe drugs for you based on what you told them about your past experience with drugs. They don't know how far you've gone in your head; remember, drug addiction is a psychological and mental sickness. Your mouth produces little information at the time you were sitting at the doctor's table. In fact, very little information will come out of your mouth. You can never compare it to what is going on in your head and mind at the moment you were talking to your doctor.

Doctors will only advise you with the information you gave. They cannot scan your brain to know what exactly is going on in your head, because you don't have brain damage. For example, I've seen some addicts say they feel like shooting the doctor who was supposed to help them with a drug treatment, all because they didn't get their way in treatment. Doctors prescribe what they feels is reasonable according to the information given and the tests carried out.

I thought I observed that alone. I didn't realize that even the addict noticed that. His opinion was that his doctor was not doing his job properly, that the doctor got him more addicted on different kind of drugs instead of getting him off the drug he was addicted to. The addict said so many horrible things about his doctor; something like the doctor was incompetent, that his license should be revoked.

But I knew he was talking out of frustration. Doctors are doing the best they know how. I perceive that he was tired of using drug but doesn't know how to beat them. He said he regretted every day for touching the drugs the first time.

Your treatment has to start from your mind and from the way you think. If your treatment has been forced by someone else, such as a parent, your spouse, relatives, or friends, it will not work, because they are trying to force you off drugs. They want you to get stable on treatment, but nobody can do that but you. The truth is no one can force anybody to do anything, especially in treatment. Man is a spirit, not a physical body. No one can force you to go through treatment.

Treatment has to start from you, not your doctor; you need to believe first that you will live your life without drugs, before any help offered can work. When you believe in yourself, it's step one, and the beginning of your freedom from drugs.

You may even feel like doing the worst while seeing your doctor, because you are not happy on the kind of dose he placed you on. Your doctor is only trying to help with his knowledge and experience with drug addiction treatment when you sought his help. You should not fight him or say nasty words about him because he didn't get you where you are right now.

Doctors are only trying to help, and they can only offer what they know. You can't blame them for what they don't know how to do. Stay calm and be positive, behave nice to everyone, invite God into your life, and let Him help you instead of being sad and bitter.

Doctors are one of those professionals that do not really believe in the supernatural. It's because of the kind of job they do. They have to see before they believe, which is what their profession has turned out to be, except for a few who were Christians before they become doctors.

In God, you need to believe before you see, forget about what you have learned in school; God is beyond your school. You can't really get accurate knowledge without God. Any doctor or professor that doesn't believe in God is a fool; the Bible has confirmed it a long time ago in Psalm 14:1 (NKJV), "The fool has said in his heart, '*There is* no God.'"

Imagine a foolish doctor treating you, or a foolish professor teaching you in school, what will you turn out to be? Likely a foolish one likes them. If you walk with a wise man, you become wiser, and work with a fool, you become more foolish than your teacher, because a seed produce more of its kind. A seed of foolishness produces more foolishness, and a seed of the wise produces more of its kind.

Wake up! There is God in heaven. He is a Spirit, and He knows all things. He sees you but you can't see Him. Don't be in the dark anymore, come to the life of light. Stop feeling sorry for yourself; stop regretting taking drugs in the first place. Stand up and make up your mind that no matter what, you are getting off drugs.

Most drug addicts are on the wrong treatment, which they are not aware of; because when the diagnosis is wrong, it is sure that the treatment will be the wrong one. Some stay on the wrong medication for years and become addicted to it. How sad.

The reason for wrong diagnoses is due to the information you provided, which will decide the prescription and the tests your doctor orders for you. Your doctor will treat you based on what you told him/her about your experience with drug abuse, and if it's not always accurate, this is what leads to wrong decision. As a result, you end up with wrong medication.

The sad thing is that you can be hooked on that wrong medication for years without realizing it. Some people don't know how to get off prescription meds. It's not doing them any good; it's making their health worse. Addictions to prescribed drugs are handcuffs that can never be removed except with the help of the Holy Spirit. You may laugh that it's not true, but it is the bitter truth. No doctor will tell you that, because they've been trained to trust their knowledge (their intellects). You know it's very hard for that kind of profession to trust God because of their work; very few believe in the supernatural.

Chapter 6
THE SUPERNATURAL LIFE

People ignore or do not believe that there is a supernatural life, which supersedes the natural life. The truth is there is something more than this physical world.

Back in West Africa, where I grew up, not too many people went to the hospital for any medical reason. Whenever someone got sick and it lasted more than a month, they believed it had a spiritual basis, meaning it required more than the normal cure and care they had put in, so they consulted the spirit through their gods and goddesses to learn what to do next. It worked for some but not many. I won't go into details because I don't want to discuss how the devil cures. I know the devil won't give you anything for free. Only God gives free gifts. All I want you to notice is the knowledge and recognition of the spirituality and supernatural aspect of it.

They did what they could, and it wasn't working, so they consulted the supernatural for healing, knowing the supernatural supersedes their own wisdom; they respected that, and it may be temporal, but it works.

Some even consult the spirit for their business and security; they believe they can be successful first through their consultation of the spirit in their business before they advertise it. They look for security first in the spirit before they employ bodyguards. They know bodyguards have their limit—they can't guard them whenever they're alone or sleeping.

How did they know there was something that could work more than their own wisdom? Most of the time there was no physical contact, nothing to drink, nothing to eat—they talked to the air, and what they asked for immediately came to pass.

I was a kid when I saw those scenarios, and I called it "talking to the air." But back then they knew they were talking to Spirit, not air. I was ignorant of that fact. They knew some power superseded the physical, and most of them respected and revered the power they did not see. They believed that anything locked in the spirit realm can't be opened in the physical; they believed they had to unlock the health of the sick person in the spirit realm first, before their efforts could work. The same applied to their businesses and everything about their lives. If not, they would be laboring in vain. They knew they couldn't go from the physical world to the spirit; it has to be from spirit to physical. They knew they were on the right track in everything they were doing.

It's the same with God's children. we have to settle things from the spirit realm before we start anything here in the physical world. I believe that if you have Jesus in your life, you are a child of God. Many of God's children struggled with prescribed drugs. Don't let any doctor put you in "life jail" that God did not put you in. When Jesus was going home, He said, "Peace I give unto you," and nothing else, Wake up and see what God has given you.

Our ignorance of this spirit realm will not allow us to access all what we have in the spirit because we don't know. God has a lot of goodies for us if only we know, and then we can have it. But if we don't know, we can't even think about it, let alone want to have access to it. It's only what you know you'll want to have, if you don't know nothing can be done.

It is very sad for someone to die as a pauper, and after his death, his friends and family discovered he was a prince, with a lot of money in the bank. How sad would that be? At the same time, it's a lesson for the rest of the family and friends to learn from.

Do not sleep in the dark anymore; life is controlled from the spirit world.

There are supernatural healings; it supersedes natural healing. That is why it is called "super" natural. You can be healed from addiction supernaturally without any medication. You can't see when the healing takes place; you may not even feel it, but you will know, it's all based on the trust and faith you have in God. It's based on your own personal faith, not mine, not your parents', or your grandparents', or your priest or pastor, or your spouse and children.

God responds to your faith because salvation is very personal. None of your relatives or friends are going through the pain of addiction with you; your faith in God is for your own good. It's better to have faith in God than to put trust in your doctor because they have no good to offer in the case of addiction.

Proverbs 3:5–8 (NKJV) says, "Trust the Lord with all your heart, and lean not on your own understanding; In all your ways acknowledge Him, and He shall direct your paths. Do not be not wise in your own eyes; fear the Lord, and depart from evil. It will be health to your flesh, and strength to your bones."

If you can be humble enough to trust God once and for all, you will be free from drug addiction. Forget what you've learned or knew already. Get on your knees and say, "God, here I am, your handywork. Help me to get free from this drug addiction; I am fed up, and I want you to take absolute control of my life. Fill me with your Spirit, so that I can know what to do next."

I'll tell you, if you do that with a genuine heart, your problem will be solved. God will not only forgive you, He will fill you with His Spirit to help you, and show you what to do with immediate results.

God doesn't waste time. He is not like doctors who will place you on long-term medications. His own healings are instant and perfect by His word. The word of God is your medication, and the Holy Spirit is your helper. He will help and remind you when and where to take your medication.

All you need to do is to ask the Holy Spirit to help you, and He will do beyond what you can even think of, or imagine. He is so gentle and loving; He loves you more than yourself. He knows everything about you, and He is the true helper. He is the doctor of all doctors. He knows how to remove your drug addiction in a second.

Remember, He created and owns you, He can take one nerve off your head in less than a second, and you stop craving drugs. That will be the end of any drug addiction in your life. You may think you have gone too far with your addiction, that you can't achieve anything good with your life—after all, no one will want to employ a drug addict, thinking nothing good will ever come out of you! No! Don't think that way. When you genuinely come to Christ, He doesn't see your mess. He cleanses you of that mess of drug addiction.

The Holy Spirit Is the Real Deal

The good news is that the Holy Spirit does not record your past when you invite Him into your life. You are as new as a newborn baby, a new species. He sees you as a champion going places.

When you realize that you can start dreaming again, you can achieve anything you want for God's kingdom and for you. Glory to God! Even though you don't see what has changed physically when you receive the Holy Spirit, something has happened in your spirit. You will know that the burden of drug addiction has been lifted. You will suddenly feel the lightness in your body; the joy and peace of the Lord will spring up in your spirit. Instantly you will know that you are free from any form of drug addiction.

It now up to you to forgive yourself and see yourself the way God sees you. If you could only see yourself the way God sees you in His word, your problems have been solved. You can start dreaming big, and there is nothing you can't achieve. No power from the pit of hell can hold you bound with drugs addiction ever again.

Whom Jesus make free is free indeed; there is nothing the devil can do about it. Satan will watch you walk away from drug addiction for free—no charge, and no stress.

Chapter 7

Your Mouth, Your World

Your mouth control your world. It put you where you are right now. What comes out of your mouth is more important than the food you eat. Your talking right will help you a lot during your natural treatment of drug addiction.

Start freeing yourself from drugs first from your mouth. What you say designs your life, and it is very important that you know that. The Bible says in Proverbs 18:21 that life and death are in the power of the tongue, and those who love it will eat its fruit. Believe in yourself, and speak positive words to your life.

Don't say you don't know how to get out from under drug addiction, and never look down on yourself. So many people have cursed themselves unknowingly with bad languages; they think it's a fashion, and the angel of darkness has already stamped what they said about themselves, so they wonder why their life is stuck in one place. They don't move backward or forward, they don't pass or fail, and they are in one place for decades.

The sad thing is, they think it is their destiny, that God put them there, and if God wants, He will remove them from where they are and put them in another place.

The reality is that God does not put anyone anywhere; your mouth put you where you are right now. And if you don't like where you are, put yourself where you want to be using your mouth. No one will do that for you, so learn to talk yourself up.

Treatment starts from your mouth before you will see the manifestation in your body. When you speak positively about yourself, you're actually talking to spirit, you are connecting to spirit world all the time, and angels execute all that you are saying. By speaking to yourself, you send your angels messages to do things for you, so they carry out what you're saying.

The same goes for all those negative words you have said! Some angels of Satan have already carried those words out for you, which is the reason for getting stuck on drugs for years without realizing it.

Put your mouth where you want your life to go, and speak what you want to see happening in your world, but don't be a negative talker. What you say is what you get in your life, and if you say nothing, you still get all negatives, so don't think that because you say nothing, you are a quiet type—you will get nothing. No, a thousand time no, you will get something you didn't want because you didn't speak out on time.

Don't speak only positive words when everything is good, then, after you turn around and start cursing yourself problems when you have little challenges. Challenges make you strong. How can you testify if you don't have anything to challenge you? Know that drug addiction is not something you can treat like a headache or stomach pain.

Imagine you are taking medication for a headache or stomachache every day. It's definitely not normal; it has to be something serious to look into, more than the pain you think. Likewise, drug treatment is more than what you are treating; it is more spiritual than physical. Treat your spirit first, because man is a spirit, not a physical body. Start the treatment from your human spirit, and then it will manifest in the physical.

You will be wondering how you treat your spirit. It's very simple, and with no cost at all. You contact your spirit with your mouth; I am talking about your human spirit—you treat your human spirit with your mouth. By speaking positive words to yourself, you build your human spirit strong, especially with God's word. But if you're full of negative words, your spirit will be weak, and before you know what happened, you're dead.

When your spirit is weak, your body can easily give up, and that is the major reason for committing suicide. So many drug addicts commit suicide because of a weak spirit, and some overdosed and think they can't continue living. This is the strategy of Satan, because he knows when your spirit is weak and takes advantage of it. Satan knows when the spirit of fear of life rises like giants to dominate you, all because of your words, which is the reason for giving in to suicide.

With my research and experience in drug addiction services, this is what addicts do most because of their weak spirit. I never saw anyone come out free and clean with the treatment the government has provided, going from one medication to another. I thought this was not the right way to live; there must be something more to this drug treatment. I realized most of them put themselves where they are now with their mouths.

The habits they formed were stamped from the spirit world, so no medication can cure them except the power of God. And your mouth has to make the power of God work in your life.

The Word of God, the Fastest Cleanser

The word of God is the fastest cleanser; it cleanses your spirit, soul, and body from all negatives and will build them up; no demon of fear can destroy you. When you are built up with the word of God, you are free for life; you are no longer in bondage.

The word of God is your life. God already told us to choose it, so we may live a life of victory in all circumstances. But sadly, drug addicts have killed themselves with their own mouths by declaring wrong words upon their lives before committing suicide.

Suicide doesn't happen in one day. It's been decided a long time ago—the first time you jokingly said you would kill yourself, that was the day Satan "demon"-stamped your word in the spirit realm. You carried out the mission when you overdosed.

Life and Death

The Lord declared in <u>Deuteronomy 30:19</u> (NKJV), "I have set before you life and death," and He said you should choose life.

He actually told us what to choose; isn't it amazing? It's like when a teacher gives students an exams, and at the same time gives them the correct answers. That is the kind of God we serve. He will give you the test and the answers at the same time.

The only thing He requires from us is to be very courageous; He wants us to be fearless irrespective of any obstacle, knowing He's always there with us. When we have that consciousness that He is alive in us, faith rises like a giant, and nothing is too big to destroy us, not even drugs.

You can build your faith by memorizing God's word. When you know God's word, the devil can't use drugs to destroy you or your family again. The Holy Spirit will prescribe your dose of the word to take every day and will dispense to you for free.

The word of God is very simple to learn when you ask the Holy Spirit to come into your life. If not, you won't really have value for it. With the help of the Holy Spirit, you respect and value the word of God more than you read the newspaper.

The word of God is God Himself, not an ordinary word; it has life in it. It can go anywhere you send it and accomplish anything you want. I remember when I was growing up, back in Nigeria; some herbalist who called himself a native doctors sent words from their bedroom that he would send those words across the sea, maybe to someone in another country. Whatever he said to someone in another country and called the person's name, those words came to pass immediately. The person knew that whatever the doctor said was done, he had no doubt about it; they all have so much conviction in the demon they were serving.

For example, if they want someone to run mad, I mean have real mental problems, not knowing what he's doing, an herbalist may be somewhere in Africa, and the person he wants to do the evil to is in America. But once the herbalist puts his concoction together and speaks those devilish words or some kind of incantation into that concoction and blows it into the air right in his bedroom somewhere in Africa, the bad words he sent to America will deliver instantly and accomplish what he said in his bedroom in Africa.

The guy in America will run mad, and there was no physical contact; now tell me, how do you want to diagnose that? Or how do you think the doctor would diagnose that kind of mental illness? The guy has no medical history; he was sound and healthy before those bad words met him wherever he was before that sickness.

It was obvious the doctor was going to prescribe the wrong

medications, which may eventually kill the man, because he didn't know the cause of the sickness and would never know until the man finally gave up ghost. Maybe not even then. The doctor will tell the guy's family lie upon lie because he'll have to come up with something while having no clue what went wrong with the guy.

Only a few doctors are filled with the Holy Ghost, and they know the case is not medical, that it's not diagnosable through medical equipment. The Holy Spirit is a teacher, and He will tell them straight that the case has to be by His word, not by their own intelligence. You don't study that in medical school unless you come to Holy Ghost school.

To be realistic, if someone can send words to another person, with no physical contact, in another place or another country, and the person immediately got sick, you should know the cure is not about taking blood samples or urine samples or doing x-rays. It has to be by the same spoken words that the person will be restored or healed because there was no physical contact. But this time, it has to be the right words; the other guy spoke the wrong or bad word and got results.

You too have to speak the right words to overcome the wrong words, and you will get results. The only right word is God's word.

Don't try to learn the right words anywhere but in the Bible. God's word is the only right word to say to yourself to accomplish whatever it is you want to accomplish. A child of God who is filled with the Holy Ghost knows all things; he knows what to do by the Spirit, because the Holy Spirit directs his steps in all circumstances; he doesn't struggle or suffer for anything.

If you can memorize God's word, it will get into your spirit by speaking it every day, and when it takes hold of your Spirit, you can't forget it again. This can help you to forget about drugs forever—it's as simple as that—but you have to focus on the word only and be disciplined. The word of God can make you change your friends and environment, especially when you are starting to learn it, which will be the only sacrifice you'll have to make.

As the word of God cleanses you from your spirit, it also builds your spirit up, and once your spirit has been built up, your soul and body will automatically follow. But if your spirit is down, there is nothing you can do to your soul and body because man is a spirit.

Your spirit is the real you. Once your spirit is made sound by the word of God, you don't have to struggle with drug addiction. The word of God that comes out of your spirit will automatically cleanse you from the inside out, which means from your spirit all the way to your body, so you won't crave any kind of drug ever again. The word of God has power, and it's potent enough to change you from a chronic drug addict to a clean person; like a newborn baby, you'll be surprised how your whole life will be reborn.

Chapter 8

TAKE THE WORD OF GOD LIKE YOUR METHADONE

In Ireland, methadone is the only accepted medication for treating drug addiction; it has to be taken by addicts every day to help reduce or replace the heroin they're addicted to.

Some addicts become addicted to this drug after leaving heroin, and some use both heroin and methadone together whenever they can't find their way with their doctor, and this sometimes results in an overdose that costs their lives.

Methadone replaces heroin to treat heroin addiction, and it's another powerful drug. When addicted to it, it can't easily detox from the system, so it's another deadly drug that is perhaps as bad as heroin.

The whole idea of methadone is to forget heroin, so it is required to be taken every day in other to stop taking heroin, but it doesn't always work for heroin addicts.

The government doesn't see anything wrong with methadone because of the money they are making on it. They have put money first, before the life of humans in addiction treatment; they don't care how many addicts are actually healing from their so-called treatment and how many are dying every year. They just want to make money.

I think the purpose of getting treatment is for you to be healed of whatever is wrong with you, but in the case of drug addiction it's the opposite. Addicts get worse after joining treatment, and they will now addicted to the replacement drug, which is hard to come off because it's a prescribed drug by the so-called medical experts.

They are making money at the expense of someone else's life. The devil offers money first when he wants to send you on an errand, and most of the time it's the money you won't be able to reject, knowing fully well that the end of it is destruction. The devil does not care about your life, he wants to deceive to destroy anyhow he knows you will give in to.

I've been working in drug treatment clinic for more than ten years now, and only one out of every hundred people really gets true detoxification, and this is only by God's grace. And it's usually when a Christian group intervenes. I have never seen successful self-detox or any successful detox from the treatment they are getting from a clinic or rehab center.

Nobody gets addicted to a drug and lives long, which means they're not fulfilling God's dream for them. Drug addiction is more of a mind sickness and is spiritual more than the physical treatment the government is lavishing money on. For example, there is no medication for preventing suicide. The only thing they will get is counseling, nothing else. It's then up to the suicidal person to accept the counseling or not, and it depends on how he feels and how his state of mind is. If his mind has been twisted by the devil, there is no amount of counseling or talks that will stop a suicidal person from committing suicide.

It's the same with drug addiction. If your mind has been twisted by the devil, nothing can be done, and you will be in treatment forever, until you die. I am not been mean, it's a fact—I've seen a lot of death, and the cause is overdose and abuse of drugs.

You can go for counseling, but it won't work because most of the time the words are empty and won't change you. Counseling will only convict you, and tell you how bad you are. It's not God's word, it is experience from some therapist.

Only when you acknowledge that life is spiritual is when your real treatment begins. You need to memorize God's word, let the word of God get to your human spirit, and it will make a champion out of you because your real self is a spirit.

You are not the body you are moving about in, you're a spirit, and you are from God. God's word is the only word that can penetrate your spirit and really make you listen to yourself before you proceed to do anything.

The word of God will open your eyes to see where you are and the way you are supposed to go. The word of God will make you listen to your real self, which is your spirit.

Therapists won't tell you what is in your mind, except you tell them how you feel and what is in your mind, but the word of God will show you the real you, who you have never met.

Talking God's word every day is better than taking your methadone every day. Methadone breaks down your spirit, the real you, while the word of God builds up your spirit. When you learn how to talk God's word every day, like the way you take your medication, you will be healed and free from drug addiction from your spirit.

I told you that the spirit controls the physical, once you are "free first from your spirit" (which I call FFFYS). It doesn't matter what your physical body reads at that moment. In fact, you may still have your medication and everything still looks the same, and you may wear dirty clothes because you've been homeless for a while now and have been sleeping on the street. Whatever your case may be, don't worry, everything will eventually conform to what the spirit wants it to be.

You may be wondering how to know you are free from drug addiction in your spirit. It's very simple. You will experience joy and peace from the inside the moment you surrender your life to Jesus, the Son of the living God. The kind of joy that will spring up from your spirit is unexplainable, and only you will experience that peace of mind. That peace will give you the confidence you have been looking for. You will have the confirmation from your spirit that you will never die of drug addiction.

My pastor always says that the word of God in your mouth is God talking. That is so powerful. I also say that the word of God in your mouth is the healing power that you need to be free from drug addiction, and it heals faster than any medication without leaving any traces of drugs.

People will not believe that you have been on drugs by the time you share your testimony; the word of God is the only cleanser that can cleanse you, not methadone. The devil studies you by your actions and words, and if you are full of negatives, cursing yourself, your life will be full of negatives and curses, and then you will wonder why things are not working for you.

If you are positive and you declare blessings on yourself every day—blessings will not elude you no matter where you may find yourself in life—this is the law of the spirit, which people refer to as natural law. The devil doesn't know what is in your mind until you say it out, and then he carries out his mission on you the moment you say negative words. Remember, every word that comes out of your mouth is a seed; it will come with multiple harvests.

You may not see it immediately after you said negative words, but it has been sealed in the spirit realm and will surely manifest in your life soon—except you can reverse it with your mouth and seal it with the name of Jesus, because the name of Jesus is an instrument given to all Christians to change anything in the spirit and in the physical world.

Your mouth put you exactly where you are right now. The life you are living is a result of your mouth, and what you have been saying from the age of accountability is what put you in drug prison. The age of accountability from my own perspective is from ten to sixteen years old, because kids have access to everything online now, so they are too smart for their age. Once a child understands the difference between right and wrong, he or she should be responsible for his or her action. You cannot in any way compare a ten-year-old in the 1960s and '70s to a ten-year-old in 2019.

I saw a ten-year-old boy already using different kinds of drugs; he started with cigarettes when he was eight (he said he used to hide and steal them from his parents out of the ashtray). I imagined that boy in my child's class and was disturbed in my spirit how he got to where he was.

The question I kept asking myself was, who am I supposed to blame? I thought he was supposed to be in school, and the only thing he should be worried about at that stage is homework. His parent should do all the worrying for him.

When I heard this boy's story my heart sank. He grew up with heroin addict parents, and all he knew was drugs. My friend said he'd been using drug right from his mother's womb. She said I shouldn't be surprised, that I shouldn't expect more from him.

But it broke my heart. I couldn't stop thinking about this little boy. I searched for a way to reach out to families like that with a good news of our Lord Jesus Christ, because I am sure that a lot of children are in his shoes. Imagine a child of ten who is already smoking and taking drugs. I wonder what he will turn to be by the time he is twenty.

I knew in my spirit that this is the strategy of the devil; he wants to handcuff youngsters with drugs before they even grow up to be responsible. He wants to render them useless for themselves, their family, and society.

Satan knows God loves little children; God spoke to Samuel when he was a little boy. Satan knows God can do great things with a child, especially from age ten. That is the reason Satan wants to hook them on drugs from that tender age, so that they will never fulfil God's calling in their lives.

One can only know all these by the spirit of God and stop blaming treatment centers for what they can't even diagnose;

people are dying every day because they lack this knowledge of truth. Your ignorant does not change what has been in existence: life is spiritual, and drug treatment is not working; it will only get you more addicted to more drugs, and that is what the devil wants. He doesn't have any job other than to destroy you.

Satan wants to blind you with drug treatment because you never thought you'd be in a drug clinic for ten years. Coming to a clinic every day for treatment has become a lifestyle, which is sad. Never consent to drug treatment as a lifestyle. It's a terrible way to live, and the end of it is death. I told you that I've never see any drug addict who did not eventually die during treatment because of an overdose. It is not that they give an overdose in the clinic, it is because addicts use more drugs outside the clinic.

God has the best way of life for you; it doesn't matter where you are coming from, or what age you are—you may be ten or sixty—it's never too late with Jesus.

Chapter 9
THE ONLY SOLUTION

Most addicts chose to use drugs for one reason or another. For example, for some people it is a family problem, for some it may be an emotional problem, or a peer group problem; only few are addicted to drugs for medical reasons.

If by any reason you have been addicted to any kind of drugs for medical purpose (such as for pain reduction), remember that Jesus is the true healer. Drugs can only reduce the pain for a short time, not cure it, but Jesus removed all our pains two thousand years ago. Believe what the Lord Jesus has done for you, so what you have to do is receive it and make it yours.

Taking more and more drugs to reduce pain leads to death. It's never the solution; it's for you to exist for a while and then die. Don't say that everybody will die one day, whether I take drugs or don't take drugs, everything will still end one day. A lady even said

I should not burden myself to preach for addicts, that something has to kill a man, that it's destined to be that way.

No. A thousand times no! I did not agree with her opinion. Nothing has to kill you except your ignorance of the truth, and the only truth is the word of God. Lack of understanding of the word makes a lot of people give in to any assumption.

That lady made the assumption that something must kill a man, but that kind of mind-set is wrong. It's hard for me to change her mind if she doesn't accept the word of God.

My own understanding of the word of God is that we can choose when to check out of this world. That is, you can choose to die whenever you want, and it's up to you, not up to God. This is another level of faith that I won't be discussing in this book. But we all know that no man lives in a body forever! But humans are spirit and can't die; they live on forever.

Remember that Christmas song that says, "And man will live forever because of Christmas day"? The song is true. I believe the writer saw the future of man through Jesus.

You can destroy your body, but you can't destroy your spirit. The spirit leaves your body and lives on somewhere forever, so don't let Satan deceive you with his tricks because he has so many. Satan is using those drugs to rub you off what God has planned for you, and that's the reason he keeps telling you that if you take drugs you will die, if you don't take drugs you will still die, and he keep telling you that, so why not do what you love and enjoy the moment?

There is no free gift from Satan. Whatever he gives you will eventually destroy you, but you will think you are enjoying at that moment. Your Spirit will tell you on your inside that if you don't stop, you will kill yourself, but you won't listen to your spirit.

You've been overwhelmed by Satan's noises, and you ignore the still, small voice because you made your spirit weak by not listening to your spirit. Your spirit is the real you, not your body; your spirit gives your body power to live and to accomplish goals.

If your spirit is week, you can't go far in life; you can only get by and live on people's opinions forever until you finally check out of this world. You can't achieve what God has planned for you, let alone help others. Everything boils down to the way you think; your mind-set is very important; your thinking makes your spirit strong or weak. You may be weak in your spirit by your thinking if you are full of negative thoughts, but your spirit can only be strengthened by God's word if you dare to learn it and put it in your heart.

When your spirit is strong, your body will be strong. There is no doubt about that, because your body will conform to what you put in your heart, and by saying it out aloud, this is a powerful medication. When you have nothing good to say to yourself, that means you don't really have God's word stored in your heart, and Satan will surely put some thoughts in your heart. He will also make you say bad words to yourself, which will weaken your spirit and your body. That is a dangerous zone to live in, and before you know what went wrong, you're already dead.

Satan will make a mess of you when you're out of your body; he will ask, since you know "the truth," why don't you follow the truth. He will quote a series of scriptures, another reason you shouldn't listen to him. Satan surely knows scripture—he quoted for Jesus as well—and he will surely do the same for you. Satan knows the truth; he wants to divert people away from it because he has been cursed and God is going to destroy him and his angels in the end. This is the reason he wants to deceive people into following him—because he knows he doesn't have a future, so he doesn't want anybody to have one.

God has planned a good life for you even before you were born; His plan is for you to enjoy your life to the maximum you can think of. Therefore, the only solution to your drug problem is Jesus Christ, the son of the living God, and you can only know Him in the word of God, not by watching the movies about Jesus but by knowing him personally and having a good relationship with Him.

Drugs don't let you live to your full potential. They make you live with sadness and guilt. It doesn't matter whether you've been taking them for a long-term disease or you got hooked out of habit. Your conflict and sadness are hard to discuss. You live with them every day, trying to disguise them with "makeup." So what's the point of taking drugs at all? Think about this: drug addiction offers a short lifespan after a useless life. Addicts rarely live to see old age. Youngsters are dying every year from overdoses. Clearly, the devil is at work. If you don't choose to be clean, nobody can help you get clean, don't let the devil deceive you into thinking a drug clinic will clean you up.

Why don't you make a U-turn and look unto Jesus the only solution? He is the author and the finisher of our faith. He is the Doctor of all doctors; He has healed diseases and infirmities that doctors can't even diagnose.

Remember the story of the woman with the blood issue in the

Bible? She didn't get diagnosed, let alone cured. Her condition grew worse, and she wasted all her money on failed treatments until she became poor. Her money was gone and her condition did not change. Thank God for Jesus—she didn't have to pay a penny to Jesus. Free consultation, free medication, and free gift—that's Jesus for you! The woman touched Jesus with faith and Jesus said her faith made her whole. You know what that means. After the woman got healed, she got all her money back and became rich again. All because she came in contact with Jesus. What a doctor!

Now tell me what doctor will treat you for free and even give you money when you tell him you don't have money for treatment. Only "Dr. Jesus" can do that. He is already loaded with riches you cannot imagine, so He doesn't need your money. You need Him more than He needs you. He has so many children functioning for Him. If you ignore Him, He won't force you. He'll turn to his other kids, who want to display His glory on earth. Not that He is looking for your faults. He wants your attention so He can bless you beyond what you've ever dreamed of.

That is the reason for sending so many people to your way to share His love with you, including me, to get your attention so that He can make you drug free and bless you in all ways. He is the only one Doctor I can recommend for you for drug treatment, because no one else will make you clean and free like He can.

If your body is sick, and the doctors have concluded that you have to be on morphine or methadone, or any type of drug to reduce addiction or pain in your body, don't give in to those lies, because you will only get more addicted to those drugs, and it won't change anything, it will only worsen your health.

So many people have died because they were addicted to morphine. It's not because they were originally addicted to drugs, it's because maybe they had problems with their kidneys, and the only medication the doctor prescribed was morphine, so they got addicted and can't come out of it until we hear the news of their death.

I realized that being addicted to so-called prescribed drugs like morphine or methadone is not helping any patient. It only makes their lives more miserable. Putting faith in those drugs is vanity. How can you trust your medication when you didn't get assurance from your doctor that one day, whatever went wrong with you will be over after taking all those drugs, and you'll be well?

In that case, you need to put your foot down and trust God. Stand your ground in faith of the Son of God, and declare His words, and as you declare God's word every day of your life, something is happening in the spirit realm, and things are shifting to their original place. The original place is to be fruitful and productive, as the Bible says in 1 Timothy 6:12. Fight the good fight of faith, lay hold on eternal life. You see, you have to fight the good fight of your own faith; this is the reason you will need to make up your mind and stop blaming everybody else for your failure.

The same verse continues to say that you should lay hold on eternal life, that eternal life is indestructible life, and you can only connect with it by your own faith, not anyone else's. Not your priest's, your parents', your friends', or your grandparents' faith will save you or make you free, only your faith will work for you.

Jesus said to a blind man in Mark 10:52 that his faith has made him whole. Look at that scenario. Jesus did not pray to the Father in heaven that "Father, please open this blind man's eyes." The blind man made up his mind that day to be free; he didn't let anyone stop him from getting his sight, nor did he make excuses for his limitations. Rather, he pursued his freedom without wavering, and he got it.

In the blind man's story, people told Jesus that the man was blind from birth. He reminded them that the man hadn't sinned. He said it is for the Glory of God to be seen. That tells me the blindness was not diagnosable, if his parents had gone to the doctor when he was a baby, which I think they must have tried. The doctors would not be able to diagnose what went wrong with the baby in the womb. They would guess and give the wrong treatment until the parents got tired and left it alone because they knew nothing would work.

Life is spiritual, my dear reader. Jesus said it is for the glory of God to be seen in the life of that blind man, that no one had sinned in his family.

Some people are like that today. God wants His glory to be seen in your life, which was the reason for going through all the challenges you are going through now, including this drug addiction. If God's glory is to be seen in your life, you go to God, not doctors, and not anybody people may suggest to you.

I believe only God is the author of Glory, and He wants that glory to be seen in you, that was why Jesus said in John's gospel (17:22 NKJV) that "the glory you gave me I have given them, that they may be one as we are one."

Look at that big gift Jesus gave us. We're not worth it, yet He gave us that much, so you can't think less of yourself, and you can't put any limitations on yourself either. Don't let any doctor put limitations of any kind on you; you can be free from drugs without any treatment with no side effects, and His Glory will be seen in your life as well, like the story of the blind man.

If you're already addicted to heroin or any kind of drugs that is harmful to the body, and you're getting treatment, thinking that it's going to get better or you are thinking that you are going to be off drugs one day, it's a big joke. Nothing is going to happen because you have allowed prescribed drugs instead of your faith to fight for you. You will only get more addicted to more drugs out there plus the prescribed ones, and the consequence of this is death—there are no two ways about it. The devil wants to use this means of treatment to destroy you before you realize the truth that no treatment is working.

It's high time you make up your mind and be determined to say no to drugs and the abuses of it.

If you want to fulfill God's calling, you have to take a bold step toward positive change. You may be thinking that you've gone a long way with drug abuse, but you can't lose hope, thinking you can't amount to anything. God did not plan that life for you.

As you are reading this book, get cleaned up and make a positive move by eating good foods. I realized that most drug addicts eat anything they see, not what's good for their bodies, because drugs have taken the most money away from them, so they end up eating junk food, and this is not healthy.

Some hardly take care of themselves; some even sleep roughly most of the time because their parents kicked them out of the house. I can't blame their parents, because drug addicts are hard to manage, especially for parents who aren't grounded in the word of God enough, even at that, they have to ask God for a "special grace" to deal with the drug addiction problem of their children. So many bad habits come with drug addiction, which can easily frustrates parents, unless they pray for that special grace.

Consciously eating good food will help you with this natural treatment of getting away from drugs. Don't wake up in the morning and start looking for energy drinks to fill up your stomach because I realized that this is what most addicts do. So eat good food, and speak the word of God to yourself, and you will realize that you can do a lot of good things for yourself without touching drugs.

Chapter 10

SOLUTIONS FOR ADOLESCENT DRUG ADDICTION

Your young faith can move mountains. God doesn't look at your size before He does big things with you. Don't waste your youth; be busy for God. Get involved in church activities, and go back to school if need be. Read and memorize God's word every day, and improve yourself in God and in you.

You improve yourself in God by studying His word every day; make sure you know at least one sentence by heart each day and use it for yourself. For example, you can memorize Psalm 23 and apply it to yourself, read it again and again until your spirit is reading it while you're asleep.

If you start on the first day of the month, by the end of the month you'll have improved yourself with thirty or thirty-one sentences of God's word. If only the one you knew in the first month of the year is the one you are declaring on yourself for the rest of the year, you made a connection with that eternal life, which is the indestructible life of God.

You will find yourself doing the right thing because joy will flow from you inside out. That is, from your spirit to your soul and body. Don't cultivate the habit of coming to the clinic every day to get medication, and after, you roaming the streets for the rest of the day, busy doing nothing. Make up your mind that you want to be drug free, and go for it by learning God's word, not by registering at an addiction clinic.

The word of God you are learning and declaring every day is redirecting your life back to what God originally made it to be, and it will plug you out from domain of darkness and into light. Drugs are a domain of darkness, so don't stay there.

The word of God you are declaring will make you think of going back to school if you need to complete your education, especially if you dropped out because of your addiction. This time, you're going back to school with joy and glory. The word will now make you to understand the reason you should go back to school.

If you don't go back to school, make sure you're doing something that will keep your mind busy. For example, get involved in the choir at your local church. If you are singing, sing well, if you are drumming, drum well, if you want to be involved in charity work, let it be from your heart and do it well.

I will advise that anything you want to settle for in life, make sure you have at least a minimum education so you can communicate well with people, because life is all about people and people only, which is what Jesus came to die for. Put your young faith to work, and you will surprise yourself at how your life will turn around with the goodness of God, and you won't need to touch drugs.

God is so big, He can remove one nerve from your brain and you will stop craving drugs, and that will be the end of drugs in your life. It will be like a dream. In Psalm 126:1, when the Lord restored the captives of Zion, it was like a dream.

So don't let drugs limit or dictate your future. You're still young and full of energy. It doesn't matter that you were born into a drug-abusing family or you got involved in drugs through your friends. You can't blame anybody for your habit, so put your little faith to work, and it will make you free from drugs forever.

All I have told you can be achieved with the help of the Holy

Spirit, who is a person like you. He is friendly and gentle and knows all about you. He is the one who will remind you of the right thing to do at the right time; you won't have to make any blunders again, and you will be doing the right thing for the first time.

Make up your mind and give the word of God a try. Use the word of like your medication: let it come out from your mouth every day. Set time for the word of God every day you wake up, as if you set time for your daily clinic. Declare the word of God at the time you're supposed to be taking your methadone.

Deliberately replace your medication with the word of God every day, and you will find your life going forward to it original plan God made for you. You can achieve a lot for God if you start living for Him when you are still young; you can dream big and achieve it as young as you are. You can accomplish so many things for God when you start early, so don't let the devil talk you out of God's blessing.

God wants you to give yourself willingly to Him—not by force or under compulsion, but by love. He wants you to realize how much He loves you and turn to Him yourself to appreciate that love.

If you know how much God loves you, your life challenges get solved, because you will not have to worry about anything. You will realize that He is your caretaker; Jesus is your carer, and He want to care for you more than you can ever care for yourself.

Put your trust in Him only and give Him all your worries, for He cares for you. Have this mentality that no matter what Satan throws at you, Jesus loves you anyway. The realization of God's love will make you do big things for Him without fear. When you're filled with God's love, there's no limit to what you can achieve, and there won't be anyone you can't talk or relate to.

This is my reason for writing this book; I see the love of God in every drug addict I have met so far, and I know they can live their best without drugs, if only they knew better.

Therefore, make up your mind today to live your best for God; don't limit yourself with drug addiction. Be conscious that Jesus loves you, and live with that consciousness every day; get to know Him more and more by studying your Bible every day, and you will be surprised by what God can do with your life.

About the Author

My name is Damilola Success, I am a Christian, I studied addiction and I worked in drug addiction clinic for more than 10yrs now. I joined addiction service with the Health board in Ireland in 26th of March 2007 precisely, and am still working with drug addicts till now.

Few months after I joined the service, Holy Spirit said to me that, "I am the light shining in the dark" I understood the phrase because we always sing it as a song when I was growing up in children's church as young Christian. But God keep telling me this anytime am working in the clinic, I thought to myself that how does these words related to my working here in this clinic.

Until God said to me again that, I am the light shinning in the dark, I thought I am to make a song out of it, but God said to me that, is not for me to make song out of it, but to show them His light in my work place especially to all the addicts, He said to me that, this is the reason He put me there, for His children to come out from the darkness of drug addiction, to see the light of God, because God is light in Him there is no darkness at all.

God want me to show every drug addicts the life He has called them to live, and He wants me to let them know that the drug treatment is just a life handcuffs that devil is using now to reap people into his kingdom.

My experience with drug addicts and the love of God in my heart make me want to give this vital information out. The reason for this book is that, in the last ten years of my work experience with drug addicts, I have never seen anyone clean up through addiction clinics, meanwhile, we are surpose to be treating them from whatever drug they were addicted to, so that they can stay clean and live a drug free life.

I have seen a lot of young stars death that is unspeakable during these ten years, yes some drug addicts were faithful to the clinic according to our policies but they still die anyhow with drugs.

I discovered by the Spirit that this treatment we are giving is not working; I concluded that, the treatment is not the answer to drug addict problem and it will never solve the problem of any addiction either.

Printed in the United States
By Bookmasters